BROKEN WINGS:

A COLLECTION OF POEMS

By:

Kristan Key

GOLDEN AVENUE

PUBLISHING

For the people out there who feel alone, who feel unwanted, and who feel like they are losing their battle to the darkness of their minds:

You are _not_ alone.

You are _not_ unimportant.

You are _not_ a waste of space.

Fight to stay here, because you _are_ loved.

ACKNOWLEDGEMENTS

Huge thanks to everyone who has supported me in the last several months as I've put together my first two books. Without you all, they'd still be collecting dust.

To my mother, for telling me I could do anything I set my mind on. To my grandparents: Diane, Jeff, Harold, and Charlotte – I love you all so much.

To my oldest friend, and person who knows me better than I know myself, Justin: You ditched me for the Florida sun, but that's okay, I forgive you.

For my good friends: Cori, Laura D., and Laura C., without your support, I'd just be a girl sitting in front of a computer screen, wishing she could write a book.

My love to you all.

"DANCING WITH DARKNESS"

A darkened night,

world devoid of light.

A girl walks alone

trying to atone.

It's nothing that she did,

it's just because she is

different.

She must rely on herself

to take away her own sadness

by bringing light to the world

where she finds only madness.

Tears stream down her face,

but she must move forward.

The darkness is gaining,

always waiting for her.

One step ahead,

two steps back,

three skips one way,

she's losing track.

Sunlight breaks through the trees,
just a bit that she can see.
But it's there with an unspoken call,
to give her hope when she feels small.
It's okay, it says – to be different.

"CAGED BY SOCIETY"

So, you've got some extra lovin'.

Most women do.

Perfection is a fallacy,

no matter what magazines tell you.

The beauty is in being different,

not in being the same.

Love yourself in the skin you're in,

don't play society's game.

They tell you that to fit in you should be
small,

with super model height at 6 feet tall.

Your skin should be clear,

your teeth should be straight,

if you don't contour - you won't get a
date.

Your lashes should be curled,

your cheeks should have blush.

Don't forget to draw in those brows, girl,

go all in or bust.

If you have acne, that's okay, just conceal it.

Put more makeup on your face,

that's society's tip.

You need to lose weight?

Just start eating less,

maybe don't eat at all

so you can fit in that dress.

Wrinkles near your eyes?

We have creams for that.

We'll do anything to stop natural aging,

like Botox, face lifts,

… it's all a trap.

They make you not like yourself

the way that you were born.

We're losing ourselves piece by piece

without realizing it's a cause to mourn.

You are incredible just as you are,

with every little one of your scars,

with every little part of you that makes you stand out.

Love who you are,

it's what life is about.

"NOT YOUR FAULT"

"Oh my," she cried

with a tear in her eye.

As her heart began to pound

she stared at the cracks in the ground,

thinking of her past

and how she's allowed the pain to last.

It was NEVER her fault.

These things happened to her,

and it's sad, that's true.

It's kept her up at night

wondering if she's been a fool.

It was happenstance,

perchance,

that it happened to her,

and not to some other poor young girl.

"Oh my," she cried again,

realizing then,

that the pain she's suffered

could've been her end

if she hadn't been so strong

and fought to hold on

when the world looked like nothing

but black.

"No more," she wept,

the tears falling fast.

"No more will I be haunted by my past.

It's not my fault that this happened to me.

It's not my fault," she said

one more time,

wiping her eyes

and looking to the sky.

It was NEVER her fault.

"BLINDNESS CURED"

Sadness, feelings, mixed emotions,

I'm breaking free from this misguided
devotion.

We're family, or so I thought,

but family doesn't leave family to rot

in a place so dark and cold they can't get
out,

and you just watch and laugh as they're
breaking down

into dust.

Your words are like razorblades across my
skin,

my skin, so thin.

They slice and dice and do their damage,

wreaking havoc and mayhem and adding
baggage

to an already full suitcase.

I've always wondered what it is I've done.

If it's because I'm the daughter who flies
too close to the sun.

Letting the light in,

and forcing out your dark.

Realizing that you have nothing more than
your bark,

to hurt me.

Despite your attempt to decimate my
character

by spreading lies and gossip that depict a
false caricature

of who I am, I remain true.

Sadness, feelings, mixed emotions,

I'm breaking free from this misguided
devotion.

You can try to stop me, but I don't think
you will.

It's too easy for you to hate,

or simply not feel.

So, I'm sorry,

not though, in the way that you're
thinking.

I'm sorry that your heart is hardened and
sinking

further away

into a deep blue sea.

Where light cannot touch,

where love cannot be.

"STEREOTYPICAL MAYHEM"

We have to fight

the stereotypes

that try to hold us down.

We should not,

nor should we ever have been

classified before we begin.

Placed in a box

based upon race,

based upon gender,

based upon face.

Go get a frappuccino, white girl,

purchase it with privilege.

Take another selfie girl,

put a filter on that image.

It doesn't matter who you are,

putting classifications on others is

going too far.

You can't judge a person's heart by

the color of their skin.

The color of skin is no indication of sin.

The only way to know is to look at their
actions,

pay attention closely

before you cause any traction.

Just because I'm white,

doesn't mean I'm basic.

We look the same underneath,

it'd be easier if you'd just face it.

"THE CHASM"

Cracks, cracks,
broken glass.
Shattered mirrors,
a pain that lasts.

Whispering,
screaming,
it's growing louder.
Your calm blows away
like translucent powder.

Panicking, panicking,
you need to get free!
You're dying inside,
can no one else see?

Run, run,
faster, faster.

Danger is lurking,

it's pulling you backwards,

ripping at you with maniacal laughter.

You will never get out.

You're tearing at the walls again.

The walls, the walls,

the walls of your skin.

Fingernails breaking,

your whole world is quaking,

your soul for the taking.

You will <u>never</u> get out.

"HEY THERE, SWEET STUFF"

Hey baby,

what's your name?

Come a little closer,

let me see that pretty face.

How old are you?

Wanna hook up?

How much do you weigh?

What size is that bra cup?

Do you have Snapchat?

What about Tinder, or Kik?

If you're looking for a good time,

you're my type of chick.

Where did we go wrong in society

for people to think this is okay?

To treat young girls and women

like they're pieces of meat

on a silver tray?

These are daughters, sisters,

cousins, and mothers.

Would you treat your own family this way?

As you do to another?

You need to change your way of thinking.

In fact, the whole world does.

Learn to adjust your way of speaking,

if not for your family, do it because:

Young girls are growing up believing their value

is in their face,

when it's really their MINDS that matter,

not the size of their waists.

Constantly sexualized, generalized,

vulgarized, and demoralized.

They're seeing these things through

impressionable eyes.

So take a minute

and think about what you're going to say.

This could be your sister, daughter, or mother

being treated this way.

"DROWNING IN DEPRESSION"

I'm underwater.

Drowning, drowning.

My fingertips are reaching

but I just continue sinking.

I live down there,

in the dark, in the deep.

I try to escape

but I can't swim free.

It's a dungeon-less dungeon,

a cage for my mind.

I'm desperate for light

I can never find.

I'm terrified.

I've seen things down here.

The darkest recesses of my soul

leaves me shaking in fear.

Monsters in the form of thoughts,

snarling and ravaging

as the best of me rots.

Eyes peer down

from somewhere above;

pitying eyes

hidden by love.

They put on their wet suits

and jump into the pool,

but refuse to go to the deep end

where all my demons rule.

After a while, they get tired of waiting.

I try to swim up with them

but their light is quickly fading.

I'm underwater.

Drowning, drowning.

I live down there,

in the dark, in the deep.

I try to escape

but I can't swim free.

"YOUTHFUL IGNORANCE"

Let's go party.

Let's get drunk!

Let's go wild with pills and drugs!

We need to be intoxicated

to have fun.

This world will never tame us.

That closeminded thinking

will get you into trouble,

when you're trapped in

a downward spiraling bubble.

It's okay to have fun

when you're young,

but you need to be smart

before someone who loves you

is forced to suffer a broken heart.

When you're buried underground,

the world above you continues.

And all that's left is the sound

of a 'died too young' tribute.

You. Are. Not. Invincible.

"SPRING"

Golden red rays filter through the trees,

the flowers below swarming with bees,

there's a smell of honeysuckle floating on
the breeze.

Welcome, welcome

to the beginning of Spring.

Birds whistle sweet songs to each other

as they build nests to offer their babies
cover.

They fly high in the sky

to glide and to hover.

Welcome, welcome

to the beginning of Spring.

Caterpillars cocoon and begin to molt

into these creatures that are beautiful to
behold.

Their lovely colors are incredibly bold.

Welcome, welcome

to the beginning of Spring.

Children are running outside

and they're laughing,

playing some game their adults might find baffling.

But that might make it all the more fun,

as they continue chasing and playing in the sun.

Welcome, welcome

to the beginning of Spring.

"BEHIND THE SMILE"

Sometimes I look in the mirror

and I can't recognize myself.

I think:

Who is that woman?

Why is she so sad?

Years and years of being told she's not
good enough.

Yo-yo dieting,

and severe depression have gotten her here.

Trapped

in her own body.

The pounds keep mysteriously appearing.

Wrinkles near her eyes,

sleepless nights,

she's only 25.

Her youth stolen away by people

who don't even realize they'd stolen it.

They took it from her,

with their cruel words

and lack of love.

She's fending for herself now,

and she's failing.

She wishes she could just curl up in a
ball,

and disappear.

Lights out.

No one would know.

Months would pass,

and no one would know.

Eventually the landlord would show up

looking for his rent.

He'd find her and say,

"Looks like we got another one."

Cut his losses, and call it in.

No funeral.

Who could afford that?

A plaque is made in her honor.

"Sister, daughter,

died too soon."

Who was she?

Not anybody important.

Gone, she's gone,

becoming a distant memory.

A few tears would be shed,

and then they'd remember…

Well, we didn't really know her in life,

so what's the point in crying for her
death?

And the world would continue turning,

and the lives would continue on,

and the landlord would find a new tenant.

Who was she,

but a whisper in the wind?

Sometimes I look in the mirror

and I can't recognize myself.

I think:

Who is that woman?

And why is she so sad?

"THE VIRGIN QUESTIONS"

You're HOW old? And you've NEVER had sex?!

Is there something wrong with you?

Did you lose a bet?

There's obviously something,

I mean, that's just not normal.

You must be such a prude,

or have reeeeally high morals.

Are you disfigured?

Is there a physical anomaly?

Because normal girls don't wait that long,

I lost mine when I was thirteen.

Are you a psycho?

Do you have a lot of baggage?

What could've happened to you

to cause all that damage?

Sure, I regret losing mine so soon,

but to wait THAT long?

You're obviously a loon.

I mean, why don't you just get it over
with?

It's not that big of a deal.

Just go out and give it to whoever will
take it.

Let them cop a feel.

It doesn't mean anything,

I mean, it's just your body.

After a while, trust me, girl,

sex will be a hobby.

You're HOW old? And you've NEVER had sex?!

Is there something wrong with you?

Did you lose a bet?

"DADDY ISSUES"

Little girl, little girl,

your daddy doesn't love you.

He's got a new family,

he's got a new daughter,

and they will always be above you.

Shh, stop crying,

you little baby.

The world doesn't revolve around you.

Didn't you hear me say stop it, already?

There is no love to surround you.

Little girl, little girl,

growing up with all this pain.

She's so alone, so alone

her faith in family

disappearing,

only bitterness remains.

She's standing outside

looking in.

Their light is so bright

and she's become dim.

Little girl, little girl,

your daddy doesn't love you.

He's got a new family,

he's got a new daughter,

and they will always be above you.

"BLOOD SO RED"

Cut me open,

and you'll see I'm bleeding inside.

Biology aside,

my heart is torn.

Jagged pieces.

And it's me.

It's all me.

The pot finally recognizing that

the kettle is black.

Something's wrong.

Innate.

Within.

Empty.

Wanting to die,

rather than live.

Pointless.

Is this all there is?

All I am?

Alone.

They always go

and never stay.

Ripping at my skin.

I want out.

Crazy.

Bat-shit crazy.

Two of me;

one is good,

she wants to fight.

But she's so tired.

Fighting is hard

when you're fighting all the time.

Exhausted: she's at her worst.

That's when the *other* sneaks in.

Whispers: "You're not worth it.

Nobody cares, nobody loves you.

Go ahead and disappear.

Go ahead and let it go.

You're ugly, so… so ugly.

No talent, not special.

Nobody wants to hear what you have to say.

Cut, cut, cut. Just try it.

Not side to side, down the middle, like you mean it."

**STOP IT. STOP IT. STOP IT. GET OUT OF MY
HEAD.**

PLEASE. Please.

Crying and hanging on by painted pink
nails.

Façade as fresh as yesterday and the day
before.

Masked, a raging war within.

Good one, bad one, which will win?

Every day, slipping closer to the edge.

Why haven't I jumped yet?

What's worse than being alone?

So,

cut me open,

and you'll see I'm bleeding inside.

"WHAT DO WE DO WHEN WE FALL?"

So you fell.

You fell!

Big deal,

get up!

It's embarrassing, yes.

Do you wish you can hide?

Would you prefer to be alone

so you can sit there and cry?

Is the shame SO much,

you just <u>cannot</u> bear it?

Is your life now over

because of this catastrophic moment?

No, it's not.

Life DOES move on.

This split second in time

will eventually be gone.

It'll be a memory,

yes, a memory.

A piece of the past.

Who knows?

Maybe one day,

it may make you laugh.

It's the way you get up after you fall,

so get up.

GET UP.

GET UP,

and stand tall.

"SELFIES ON POINT"

Selfies here, selfies there.

Selfies, selfies

everywhere.

It doesn't matter where you go,

you have to snap at least one photo.

If you don't, the people will know,

your life isn't all sunshine and rainbows.

Selfies here, selfies there.

Selfies, selfies

everywhere.

In a plane, on a bus,

in the bakery buying cinnamon buns.

Before class, in class, after class too.

If you don't post a selfie, no one will
know you're at school.

In the bathroom, on a date,

because of the bathroom selfie, you were late.

Perfect hair, just the right angle.

Your selfie game is on point!

Ooh, is that a selfie with a bagel?

At the doctor, at the dentist,

in the gym while you're flexin'.

In the park, in the zoo,

all the animals are staring at you.

In the grocery store, in aisle three,

you NEED to take a wheat bread selfie.

56 selfies you do, per week,

all because those brows are on fleek.

Selfies here, selfies there.

Selfies, selfies

everywhere.

"THE WATERS"

The waters, they're rushing.

Rushing, rushing.

The waters, they're rushing.

Non stopping,

unrelenting.

They're swift, they're fast,

they're making their own path.

The waters, they're rushing.

Rushing, rushing.

They break whatever holds them

with sheer force and power.

So strong, so mighty

but that can change in an hour.

They're so inviting, so enticing.

Come on, dear, take a dip.

But be careful,

they may push you

just enough to make you slip.

Soon you'll be travelling fast

down a slippery slope

with nothing to hold onto.

So, be careful,

Mother Nature

can come back to haunt you.

"THE SNAKES WITHIN"

I'm not afraid of the dark.

I'm afraid of what lies within.

The monsters hiding

inside of those that act so prim.

They slither,

they hiss,

they'd tear you to bits.

With one little kiss,

you're trapped.

"Trusssst ussss,"

they whisper,

enticingly suspicious.

"Trusssst ussss, dear girl, your ssssoul
sssmellsss delicioussss."

They're lying in wait

to attack behind your back.

You may never see it coming,

so cover your tracks.

I'm not afraid of the dark,

I'm afraid of the false.

The two-faced monster

on which negativity calls.

"CHANGE IS COMING"

The trees whisper to me,

softly, gently.

The breeze rustles through my hair,

as if to say,

"Change is coming."

I look out,

beyond myself, beyond the landscape,

beyond the earth, beyond the universe

and wonder.

What is death, truly?

Death of a pet, a person, of a dream?

What is death?

Is it truly an ending?

Or is death just a word we use because we
have to

categorize and compartmentalize

the things that truly mystify?

The trees whisper to me,

softly, gently.

As if to say,

"Change is coming."

"I DON'T BELIEVE YOU"

When I was young,

you told me that my dream

was infallible.

Rejectable,

impossible,

and altogether laughable.

You spit in my face

your words of discouragement.

Change your dreams,

change your wants,

change yourself.

"Maybe you should do something more
realistic."

As if what I had been dreaming

was a lie I made up.

Too illiterate to be a writer.

Too unattractive to be on film.

You told me when I was young
that my dream was infallible.
Now I'm telling you,
nothing is impossible.

"TO BE A CHILD"

Once, you were a child.

Before innocence was ripped away,

before there were hands,

hands,

touching hands

that don't belong,

that shouldn't be there.

Once, you were a child.

Before friendships were lost

over your embarrassment.

Before there were eyes,

eyes,

judging eyes,

looking at you like you're a liar.

Once, you were a child.

Before insecurities settled in.

Before there was fear,

fear,

disabling fear,

keeping you from trusting anyone or
anything.

Once, you were a child,

before all you wanted was to **be** a child.

"THE SOUND OF WINGS"

Alone, alone,

perpetually alone.

A girl with no purpose, a girl with no
home.

Flittering, fluttering

like a lost little bird,

trying to find her place in this huge
massive world.

Adrift, adrift,

constantly adrift.

A girl whose confusion blossoms as she
watches her world shift.

Flittering, fluttering

like a lost little bird.

She doesn't know what to do, she's been
told her dreams are absurd.

Aflame, aflame,

passions aflame.

She's got this need to belong, to fight
past the pain.

Flittering, fluttering

like a lost little bird.

She's learning there's nothing wrong with
being a dreamer,

or so she's heard.

Alive, alive,

wonderfully alive.

The world is a clear sky in which she can
take flight.

Flittering, fluttering

like a bird with a dream.

She flies higher and higher, her bright
wings will be seen.

"STOLEN AWAY"

Do you know

where innocence goes,

once it's stolen away?

A darkened place

full of empty space,

where children's smiles go to waste

and evil monsters like the taste

of what was once so pure.

Once it's taken

we can't get it back.

Ripped away,

leaving nothing to grasp

or hold onto.

Darkness, darkness,

goodbye light.

We've been forced to grow up too fast now,

against all that's right.

Do you know

where innocence goes

once it's stolen away?

A darkened place

full of empty space

where children's smiles go to waste.

"LOOK UP"

I look at you all

from my perch up high.

I look at you all

mosey on by.

It's easier to put into perspective

when you take a step back

and ponder for a moment

if you're on the right track.

I see all of you

and your missed connections.

Cell phones and self absorption

have all your attention.

There are people,

so many people,

passing each other on the street.

Take a moment,

look up,

you'll never know who you'll meet.

"FORGET ME NOT"

Forget me not

when I go,

because the world won't remember.

My life will be gone,

like a whisper in a breeze.

There one moment,

gone the next.

You have to strain your ears

in order to catch it,

but even then

there's no way to know

if you've heard it correctly.

But, I suppose that's normal

for most of our lives.

We're just regular people:

average Joe's and Josine's.

We're not stars,

we're not celebrities.

Our lives are not as big.

But if we can touch one person,

at least one person's life,

our name can go on

even after we die.

So,

forget me not,

when I go

because the world won't remember.

"IN THE BLUE CORNER"

Sometimes your past comes to haunt you,
in little sneak attacks.
You don't know when they'll happen,
you don't know how to fight back.

They hit you real fast,
like they're Muhammad Ali.
You can't block a hit
because you're mesmerized by their feet.

Dancing around you,
you're going in circles,
then that hit lands its target.
They call that punch the 'tear jerker'.

You're pinned in the corner,
jabs break your ribs,
you can't catch your breath,
and can't fight the hits.
Your eyesight is wavering,

the light going dim.

Flickering, flickering.

Memories always win.

"WE'RE ALL LOOKING FOR SOMETHING"

Trapped,

like a piece of garbage in the ocean,

floating without land in sight.

There's a pretense of freedom,

but how can you be free when you're stuck

in a place you don't belong?

The ocean swells and the waves overlap,

sending you spiraling out of control

and even further away from hope than you
started.

Other pieces of trash float nearby,

thrown away, unwanted.

You and they swirl together for a time,

the pressure of the water pushing you
together,

until eventually you're torn apart.

Time goes by slowly,

slower than the time it took to make you,

being out here all alone might be enough to
break you.

Then you see it.

A dark mass ahead.

You're so close,

and you can see the conglomeration of
garbage

just like you,

basking in the sun, their plastic is
glinting

like diamonds of acceptance.

They call to you, "Come here. You're among
friends."

Hope renewed, vigor restored.

You float ever closer.

Then a shadow covers you before the waves
engulf you

and you're sent right back out there,

to somewhere you don't belong.

Like a piece of garbage,

in the ocean.

"WE ARE ONE"

Fight for me,

that's all I ask.

You're the only one who can do it.

You're the one hidden beneath,

locked away,

trying to breathe.

Every time you come up for air,

you're pushed down much further than ever
before.

The good parts of us

are all tied up in you,

that's why you must fight.

We have everything to lose.

Don't give up on me,

because I am weak.

Lend me your strength,

so we can be complete.

Two sides of the same silver coin.

One side is darker than the other.

If we work together

we might just end up being

one hell

of a self lover.

"TOO YOUNG"

Anger.

Blacker than night,

blacker than black could ever be.

These people,

they hurt us,

abuse us,

mistreat us,

molest us.

We were taught to trust those we know.

Beware of people you've never met.

As if stranger danger was where true danger
hid,

and not in those around us

lurking.

Lurking,

so well, it's nearly impossible to see

these wolves hiding in the skin of sheep.

And we learn,

we learn,

safety is a fallacy.

A lie we tell ourselves so we can fall
asleep.

Although our skin is crawling

from the inside out.

So you tell,

then her eyes are crying tears of doubt.

You told,

but nobody believes you.

You're a liar, those eyes scream at you.

But you know, you know, what you're saying
is true.

You were there.

You felt the hands that don't belong

from someone you thought could do no wrong.

Oh, and the guilt.

The guilt!

The what did I do?

I must've done something to deserve this.

No, in truth,

it wasn't our fault.

It's the monsters in the minds

of those who surround us.

Breaking us, breaking us.

Forcing us to rebuild from the ground up.

We're too young

to have a hate this deep,

coursing through our veins

causing us to bleed.

"GOLDEN KEYS"

Golden keys

glistening on a pedestal.

They are your salvation,

yet you don't even know what they unlock.

Taunting, taunting, taunting.

They laugh at you,

they see you struggle.

They watch you break your back for them.

Why do you do it?

You do it because everyone else does.

Reaching, reaching, reaching.

They're just like you.

You're all following the same brick lined
assembly line.

Flashing lights,

distracting as they awe you.

Whispering, whispering, whispering.

They're convincing you of what you want

while weeding out those who question.

Outcasted for asking why.

What do the keys unlock?

Everything you've ever wanted, they purr.

The hunger is apparent in the eyes of those around you.

New car, nice house.

Money, money, money.

Eyes greened by the reflection of dollar bills.

Golden keys

glistening on a pedestal,

held in place by cast iron chains.

You don't see,

until it's too late.

"THE LAYERS"

I look at myself in the mirror. What do I
see?

I see that 5 year old girl who thought
being touched was a game.

I see that 6 year old girl who was told if
she did him a favor, he'd give her that
pretty shiny rock.

I see that 9 year old girl who went
swimming at the lake with her cousins, and
a man touched her underwater.

I see that 10 year old girl who thought she
would lose her friend if she didn't kiss
her back the way her friend wanted.

I see a 24 year old woman, still
technically a virgin, because she's
terrified.

Terrified of someone touching her, loving
her, and seeing these things about her that
she knows are so wrong.

I see a woman who replaces those
relationships with pepperoni pizza and
romantic comedies on Netflix.

I see a woman who avoids going out with
friends because she knows she's the only
one who won't be looked at, the only one
who is worthless.

I see a woman who tried dating online once,
and when he saw her, his face fell.

I see a woman who would rather sit at home
writing poetry with her cat because at
least there is no rejection there.

I see a woman who is unlovable, with her
massive thighs and rotund tummy, and a
double chin that keeps getting bigger and
bigger every year.

Self love, they preach. And she's tried.

She's tried.

But how can you love yourself if no one
else will?

"THE DARK SIDE OF THEIR LOVE"

I sit in the dark:

dark like the irises of my parents eyes
when they tell me that I should lose some
weight,

dark like the bathroom I'm hiding in so
they won't see me cry,

dark like the anger I have because they
won't just accept me.

Why aren't you more like your sister?

Your sister with the blonde hair and the
hazel eyes,

she's a cheerleader, you know?

And what are you?

Just some chubby girl in drama class with
the good grades and intelligence,

but intelligence won't find you a husband,
and neither will your ability to read
books.

Books with pages as frail and rippable as
your self esteem.

Why? Why in the world are you so tall?

You're never going to find a man and be
able to look up into his eyes.

"We don't play favorites," they chime
together.

Smiles of guiltless deception perched on
their lips,

lips that usually look like a lowercase N.

Their disapproval almost as stagnant as the
shit coming out of their mouths.

Playing favorites is their favorite game.

One of us playing Princess Peach and the
other playing Bowser,

they pit us against each other on the
Rainbow Track

while not so secretly cheering on one and
not the other.

And you lose. Of course you lose.

Because you didn't have confidence from the
start.

And their eyes gleam at their perfect
daughter, and you, you just sit there in
the dark.

"SEXUAL CREATURES"

We're taught as young girls that beauty is the end all, be all.

If we grow up to be beautiful, things will be much easier for us.

Most importantly, the men will notice you and want to give you things.

But I can attest personally that you don't have to be beautiful for some men to want to give you things.

All you need is to be vulnerable.

See, in vulnerability comes susceptibility and in susceptibility comes and inability to fight back.

It starts with them cat-calling the 9 year old girls walking in the mall.

The girls giggle and swing their undeveloped hips back and forth in a way that makes them feel uncomfortable, but hey, that's what women do in the movies.

You know they sell bikinis for little girls now?

The age of sexualization is getting younger and younger.

Molestation stories from when we were kids becoming a normalcy in society.

And yet we still strive for beauty above
brains, long legs above common sense, a
bikini body over sense of self.

Who we are is wrapped up in sex.

Who we are is wrapped up in being noticed
by the opposite sex.

Notice me, our red lips and high heels
scream. I just want to be loved!

But it's an endless circle, because the
love they want to offer involves a Motel 6
and the morning after pill,

staring at ourselves in the mirror
wondering why they didn't stay.

The makeup washes off but the hurt still
lingers.

You question why you're always the one
night stand but never the wife.

Oh, you've had prospects before, but they
always began with, "I love you because
you're so beautiful."

And you don't want to be known for just
being beautiful yet if the men don't
acknowledge you, you assume that you're
ugly and what a vicious, vicious mess
you're in.

So you lather that lipstick and slip on
those heels, and remember what you learned
as a girl.

Beauty is the end all, be all, and if you're not beautiful, just be vulnerable. That's the way to make a man want you. What else do you need?

"THE UNICORNS IN YOUR MIND"

Somebody told me once that depression is
just a figment of my imagination.

It's an attention thing, they said, with
their nose upturned and one eyebrow raised
to say:

"I caught you in your lie."

It took all I had not to smack that smirk
off of their face.

My hand shaking in anger at how completely
ignorant they are of something they don't
understand.

Figment of my imagination?

There are people in the world who believe
in the Boogie Man, and the Loch Ness
Monster,

shadow worlds, poltergeists, and El
Chupacabra.

Fortune tellers are being paid 9.99 per
minute to tell you if you'll ever find
love.

But DEPRESSION is so much harder to
believe?

That our brains might be wired differently,
causing us to be sad ALL THE TIME?

An attention thing, they said.

If I wanted attention, I wouldn't go home
and sit by myself watching TV and wishing I
could die.

If I wanted attention, I'd slap on a mini
skirt and some long black boots and quite
possibly do something

illegal.

No, depression is not a figment of my
imagination.

A figment of my imagination would be having
hope that ignorance would become a notion
of the past.

That'll happen on day, I'm sure of it.

And it'll come riding in on a rainbow,
sitting atop a unicorn.

"STAY AFLOAT"

You know you're slipping.

They don't make shoes resistant enough

to keep you from falling

off the balance beam you're twirling on

called life.

But it's more like a balance beam

on top of a seesaw,

in the middle of the ocean.

You try to stay centered,

but with every wave crash

you slide a little further.

Holding on for dear life,

you're desperate,

and desperation makes fools of us all.

You only have two options,

to stay afloat

or tumble below into an underwater rabbit
hole,

and you've been down there before

but almost didn't survive.

The darkness has tentacles you see,

that wrap around your ankles as you try to
swim away,

pulling you back down to the bottom of the
ocean.

But what else can you do?

You're so tired.

Your legs feel like they've been beaten by
a baseball bat.

That's the price of always trying to stay
positive,

when all you're doing

is slipping.

"LOOK INSIDE"

What happens when you look inside yourself
and don't like what you see?

25 years of me, me, me.

What do I want?

Always searching, never finding.

Reaching for tomorrow but not enjoying
today.

You've become a cynic,

that which you'd hoped to avoid.

Always watching the happy while never being
happy.

Staring at your reflection and getting
angrier and angrier

that their lives look so easy,

but you don't realize they have demons too.

Their minds just aren't warped to just
focus on the bad

like yours is.

Focusing, focusing

so much it hurts.

Blood vessels breaking.

Tears pour down from red rimmed eyes,

you just want to be like them.

But you don't change,

you continue to live in envy of what they have.

So angry, so bitter.

You think to yourself,

if I were prettier, thinner, smarter,

if I were a whole different person

then maybe I'd get what they have.

But that's not it.

It's inside you.

Your anger is apparent to the people around you,

subtly.

So subtly they don't even know it consciously,

but they **feel** it.

Negativity flooding from you like an unstoppable tsunami.

It's not your outside that needs to change.

It's **inside** you.

Life is not easy for anyone.

The way you see things can make you or break you.

You put into the world what you get out of
it.

So if you look inside yourself and don't
like what you see…

adapt.

Being angry will not bring you happiness,

looking inside yourself

is a start.

"THE LIGHTS GO OUT"

I stare at my reflection in the mirror.

Eyes I don't recognize stare back.

Who are you? Where did you come from?

They say age is something that sneaks up on us.

How did I get to this point?

There is no sparkle, no gleam in these eyes that had once been so youthful.

Life has taken its toll.

If I could turn back the clock of fate

and make my former self do the things

I had wanted to do, instead of had to do,

perhaps things could have been different.

Get up.

Go to work.

What is happiness?

We don't say that word here.

Do your time.

Pay your bills.

Eat your sadness.

Go to bed.

Dream of a better life.

Get up.

Go to work.

What is happiness?

We don't say that word here.

Now here I am, staring into the mirror and wondering,

ceaselessly wondering…

Who are you? Where did you come from?

What is happiness?

I turn off the light.

We don't say that word here.

"INADEQUACY"

Inadequacy is a normal fear.

Most of us feel it when others are near.

For instance, when you and your buddies go for a beer,

there's this gorgeous brunette at the bar whose got a nice rear… - view mirror, on her car. You saw her come in.

Inadequacy.

The feeling of feeling not good enough.

But who labels us with this awful word, when we try and we try until trying's absurd?

We won't stop until affirmation is procured but even then, we can't believe what we've heard.

How sad is that?

Always to feel like the worst?

Things are OK, things are fine, then someone surpasses you and your bubble bursts.

Like the girl sitting at the end of the bar.

She sees you checking out the brunette from afar, compared to the brunette she feels like fat lard.

She covers her belly and puts up her guard,
even though she really is beautiful.

We're always vying to be something we're
not, aiming for movie star looks without
movie plots.

Emanating each other as if we're robots:
it's time to press the off button and climb
out of this box,

and put together the shreds of ourselves
before it all rots.

We have to accept our differences and sew
back the pieces.

Using needle and thread, we renew our
leases

to be who we are, not living on other
people's visas,

watching each other live like we're
official scorekeepers

and wishing we could trade out all of our
interesting features.

What's the point in being the same?

If we were the same we'd wish we were
different.

We aren't born in a factory, and maybe this
reminder will eclipse it:

None of us are perfect.

That brunette hottie you're checking out at
the bar?

She's on her 5th vodka straight because she
doesn't like who she is.

Nobody treats her seriously because of her
looks.

They act like she's not smart enough to
open a book.

Beauty Queen, maybe, but she wants to be
more.

She sees the girl at the end of the bar
staring at the floor,

and wishes they could change places.

Inadequacy, you see, is inherent in us all.

It could be life changing, or it could be
something small.

Be different, be brave,

if you have the gall.

"WHERE HAS ALL THE GOOD GONE?"

So much violence.

You turn on the news and all you see is

murders, rapes, abuse, anger,

hate.

Why?

Where does this anger come from?

We flip through channel after channel of
despicable acts,

made by men, bred by men,

the blood of man

dripping as quickly as the tears of the
people

remaining as victims.

Their pixelated faces sad reminders of what
could face us

if we ever walk out the front door.

Every good story has 10 bad ones to take
its place,

shoving the positive down further and
further until it's almost nonexistent.

School shootings, gang hits, drug
overdoses,

terrorist attacks, meaningless killings

and meaningless death.

But we can't stop watching.

We're captivated captives giving killers
credence

by continuing to click until we get out
fill.

Cultivating a culture of colorful criminals

who watch the violent news

as *children*.

Why? Where does the anger come from?

"THE LOWS GET LOWER"

Sometimes I look at my life, and I wonder why.

Why was I put here?

At my lowest low, when my cup is completely empty, bone dry, no moisture in sight,

I wonder.

Why I deserve to be here while the good ones die.

Waste of space standing at the kitchen counter, knife in hand wondering how badly it would hurt to cut.

A just punishment deserved just for being born like this.

Useless – hiding in a dark room because nobody out there likes you.

Family tag-teaming together to mock you for your physical attributes.

Ugly – inside and out, a stain on an image of a golden haired family dream.

The Quasimodo hiding in the church ringing the bells yet no one notices he's hurting.

I ring the bells over and over, weighed down by my hunchback filled with self-loathing and self-hate.

Others die too young, but I haven't died soon enough.

Cowardly – I don't have the courage to cut,
I don't have the courage to die, nor do I
have the courage to live.

So I stand there staring at that kitchen
knife, frozen.

My cup so empty I'm dying from dehydration,
hoping for a bus to crash through the
window or carbon monoxide to fill my lungs,

making the decision for me.

At least it would be over.

And maybe then, the space I'd been taking
can be filled with one of the good ones.

Sometimes my lowest low can't get any
lower, especially when I wonder why.

Why was I put here?

"WANDERING HANDS"

She was a chubby little girl,

and with the way society talks nowadays

you'd assume it'd be the chubby ones that
could stay safe.

Fear crippled her, even at five years old.

When she sat on her father's lap,

her uncertainty as ripe as bacteria laden
mold,

but he never did it.

Not like the others had done,

but she still couldn't trust that the evil
poison

wasn't in his lungs.

No, trusting was for fools,

it'd been proven as time went on.

She couldn't trust men to keep their hands
where they belonged.

Five years old and already afraid,

always living in a panic, always feeling
betrayed.

So she ate, and she ate, and she ate some
more.

She pushed her feelings down with fries and
a cheeseburger.

She thought, just maybe, it would keep them
at bay.

Wandering fingers and stolen childhood;

her self-esteem being molded by
disproportioned clay.

And everyone's lives went on like normal,

everyone's but hers,

because it all becomes real if she says the
words.

Who was she supposed to talk to about all
of these traumas?

She had no one to go to,

not even the people who were supposed to be
fulfilling an unspoken promise

to keep her safe and leave her childhood
intact,

but while they were busy fighting each
other

it was stolen,

and she'll never get it back.

She's tried everything to make her life
better, always searching for the next fix.

If food doesn't work, she'll move down the
ladder, hoping she'll find something that
will stick.

From liquid courage to herbal remedies,

depression meds and powder nosebleeds,

nothing can give her back what she's lost.

Always living in anxiety, not able to
trust.

And it's sad. It's heartbreaking really,

that now she's always looking for something
to numb her feelings,

when she should've been protected.

She should've had a chance.

Instead of hiding as a child

from wandering hands.

"REJECT THE HATE"

FOR ORLANDO

The hate has always been there.

Evil thoughts swirling in the minds of
those who would do others harm.

Prejudice has been around forever

and there are people who have to live in
fear every day.

Based upon their religion,

based upon their skin color,

based upon who they choose to love.

Prejudice has been around forever.

America was built upon the backs of
differences,

but while we've moved forward in so many
ways, the hate still lingers.

Waiting.

Muslims being harassed and called
terrorists because of their beliefs or how
they dress.

African-Americans being shot and murdered
on the street, in their homes, during
church.

Children being shot and murdered in a place that was supposed to be safe, their school.

Gay and transgender people being shot and murdered for not putting a blanket definition on what is love.

The evil and madness seems to creep up on us, but in reality it's there, all the time.

Life is fleeting.

It's gotten to the point where you or someone you love

could be killed just for breathing.

We cannot turn our back on this growing acceptance of hate.

Let's fight back with love,

before it's too late.

"DON'T FORGET"

Your silence is a death trap,

please don't ever forget that.

I know it seems easier to keep it in,

but eventually you'll wear yourself thin

and no one will understand in the end.

Your silence is a death trap.

And I know, trust me, I know it's hard.

Your insides,

insides,

blackened and marred

from a pain so deep your soul is charred

and all the good thoughts are trapped
behind bars,

but believe me, your silence is a death
trap.

You worry often, that no one will
understand,

that no one will care enough to hold your
hand.

Hope falls through your fingers like grains
of sand

and your perfect ending has all been
planned.

Please listen.

Your silence is a death trap.

There is hope out there, though it's hard
to see how.

You can't see past the pain of the now,

but there are people like me, who know and
who see,

who have fought that battle, continuously.

I get the pain, and I've been in the dark.

It's always circling like a bloodthirsty
shark.

Always around, never completely gone,

but somehow, someway, I've been able to
hold on.

And so should you.

Do you know why?

Because, **you are worth it.**

So please reach out, don't be afraid.

Try to look past the pain of today.

The world is a better place with you here,

have hope whenever the darkness is near.

Your silence is a death trap,

please don't ever forget that.

According to the
**American Foundation for
Suicide Prevention,**

(https://afsp.org)

42,773

Americans died by
suicide

in 2014.

THAT IS **JUST** IN AMERICA.

YOUR LIFE IS WORTH SOMETHING.

YOU. ARE.

IMPORTANT.

If you are ever feeling like you can't
hold on, let someone know.

In America, you can call the 24 hour Suicide Hotline:

1-800-273-8255

For those of you who don't feel like you have anyone you can talk to, please email me at AuthorKristanKey @yahoo.com

You are not alone.

www.ingramcontent.com/pod-product-compliance
Lightning Source LLC
Chambersburg PA
CBHW071013040426
42443CB00007B/756